This book is to b[...]
the l[...]

ONE ROAD

by

ANGUS PETER CAMPBELL

Published by:
Fountain Publishing
Sabhal Mòr Ostaig
Teangue
Sleat
Isle of Skye
IV44 8RQ

The publishers wish to give thanks to: Sorley MacLean for the preface and for use of extracts from the poem An t-Eilean, W. W. Norton & Company New York and London for permission to use Richard Hugo's poem The Clearances, Jim Hunter and Mainstream Publishing for use of extract from Skye: The Island.

Cover drawing, design and photography by Lyndsay Mary Campbell

Typeset by Cànan Ltd, Sabhal Mòr Ostaig, Isle of Skye
Printed by Cromwell Press, Melksham, Wiltshire

ISBN 0 9520010 1 2

British Library Cataloguing in Publication Data.
A catalogue record for this book is available from the British Library.

The publisher acknowledges subsidy from the Scottish Arts Council towards the publication of this volume.

Preface

Angus Peter Campbell is amazing. His poems are strangely original and unexpected, but intense, passionate, and significant in one way or another, or indeed in two or three ways.

Very early in the book a wonderful poem of a great modest intensity, *The Sound of a Hammer*, is followed by another wonderful poem, *Eating Scones*, in which the triumphs and tragedies of history have a glorious anti-climax:

"eating scones in Katie's kitchen".

Then there is *In The Sink*, with its domestic contraction at the beginning and then a great expansion and contraction again. Between *Eating Scones* and *In The Sink* there is the wry irony of the very different *Bus Journey*.

Well on in the book three astonishing poems follow each other: *Walking The Single Track Road*, which ends with the finality of love, pity and human sympathy:

"I burn with anger
that the people are all dead";

Angus James MacDonald, and *Sons and Fathers*. The three are most moving.

Soon after them, *Saturday Afternoon* and *Indians Dispossessed* are moving or striking, or both in very different ways, as are *The Moon Tonight*, *Ag Iasgach a' Mhic-Meanmna* (Fishing the Imagination), *Shona*, and *High-Tide. 5a.m. Ord*. The rapt imagination of *Ag Iasgach a' Mhic-Meanmna* (Fishing the Imagination) and of *Shona* is gripping.

There are 100 numbered poems in *One Road*, 84 in English and 16 English translations of Gaelic poems in the book. I have mentioned about a dozen but there are many more of superlative quality, which others might prefer to some of my first choice.

Angus Peter Campbell can be direct and 'simple': he can be passionate with a list of names of people or places or of both. He can mingle that directness with an authentic surrealism. He has a very good eye and a good ear. He can never be fashionable, contrived or precious, or factitious, and he can be triumphant with daring juxtapositions which nearly always do not seem daring. Above all, he has pathos and passion for humanity from Uist to Ord to the ends of the earth.

After *The Greatest Gift* I did not expect that so soon we would have the *One Road*, which is so different and so moving.

Sorley MacLean

**For
Lyndsay**

Contents

ix

Uist 1991

One road.

A silver wheel.

A flash of red.

A flash of blue.

Me.

And you.

Beath' Ur

Rugadh mi eadar Eiseabhal agus am machair,
ball cruinn
a' bouncadh eadar tìr is cuan:

An Ear,
fraoch, cnoc is fang;
An Iar,
gainmheach, muir is cathadh;

cearcallan sìde a' frasadh air mullachan-sinc,

cathadh sìorraidh de dh'àite,

taghadh às deaghaidh taghaidh

New Life

I was born between Eiseabhal and the machair,
a round ball
bouncing between land and sea:

East,
heather, hill and fank;
West,
sand, sea and spray;

circles of weather spinning on to the zinc-tops,

an eternal spray of circumstance,

choice after choice.

New Beginnings

The horizon
is an orange streak

morning and evening.

Genesis,

the first day.

Today

It is orange over Uist,
and no light escapes the day.

A cloud,
like God's finger,
links each darkening island.

A boat is at bay.
"Name me",
"Name me", you cry,
"Name me."

Arthur, you are worth each bicycle clip you have purchased,
each tear you have shed,
each shower you've taken,
each child you've bred.

One day, in Inverness,
a man passed me on a bicycle carrying six tins of paint,
three strung on each shoulder,
He was mad, and madly happy.

Do you know what? –
I want to light a bonfire, right now,
and stand beside you fingering your hair
whilst the thing smelt, and burnt and gave heat, and warmth.

My love.

Yesterday, we had daily cleaning.

But today –
today, we have naming of parts.

Poem from Ord

Knowing you from the evening
I sense myself looking at my hands,
God's eternal etchings, Maggie in Cochabamba and you there in Inchgarvie
fearfully and wonderfully made, in the secret place

how I love you is mostly what I want to say
as the stars echo back their beautiful distress every separated night
where the huge moon hangs, sometimes eerily,
and out the darkened window tonight
I can neither see Blàbheinn nor further west, west to lovely Uist
but this room where you only have slept, and the 23 bus on the wall,
and the cross of Christ
the single purpose of this poem, all birth, all birth, all birth,
the first breath of your life, the exhalation unto this:

For to us a child is born,
to us a son is given,
and the government will be on his shoulders.

The holy child in the manger, in there, in there was all,
the first breath of your birthday and the rest unformed
except the inmost being and the glory days, ordained by God.

Another Poem from Ord

If you dreamed,
there was a child and she once saw this:
there were mountains, as blue as they say they are in Virginia,
there were three fishing boats, the glass like water, the clouds like sweets,
correct rocks, appropriate angles, the right slopes, grass, water, whitening stiles.

there was my father, sawing, and I
playing in the shavings, sweet, sweet, sweet, smell

O God

night-time and the frosty frosty lights
glitter at the Aird
and the taibhs of the car-lights (perhaps from Rhum) sweep
when I was in bed, in bed ill, and the warmth, the warmth, of the great, great back

footsteps
on the wooden stairway on the wooden stairway
footsteps
"Chaidh an dithis aca deas ann an car" ("the two of them went south in the car")
and they were seen, they were,
"a' pògadh aig a Gharadh Mhòr" ("kissing at the great garden")

this night, my love,
my toes like oatcakes on the stairway
notes of tell-tale, kiss, kiss, this night, my love, this night, my love

two lights
glittering over
out there
this night, my love, this night, my love, oatcakes in the hall, bare feet on the stairways.

Ord Sheep-Fank

1.
Stones, not-hapazardly laid,
an old iron gate, and the usual collection of wooden staves –

also, a rusted can of lager,
not Sharon half-naked but simply Tennents

and inside,
where the grass is always, always, sheep green,
green, green, grass:

it is a Sabbath afternoon.

2.
Twenty-two hours later and I've started this poem:

Skye is so March blue that all exile is real.

Skye is so March blue that I am, almost, sitting my Highers again.

Skye is so March blue that you won't believe me.

Another of those beautiful planes has gone west, into the blue.

The sea glitters
the Cuillin is snowless,
the Monday sun, the sun shines.

3.
Inside,
on that smooth green sward,

8

they clipped their lives away in semi-crew cuts:
as I leant over the stone wall
one sang 'A Seòl Gu Montreal' and another,
with winkle-pickers in his blue eyes, sang of Daliburgh dances
where Elvis reigned supreme.

4.
And suddenly they were all sheared:
the sheep, dipped and shorn,
shook, free.

For a moment, confused.

Then boldly grazing on the bald hill.

Ord Glen

Things change:
a solitary fence stob stands
in a useless field

lambs
(you'd think, by now, that traffic-consciousness would be genetic)
half-run across the road

and are still terribly deceived
when I go m-e-e-e-e-e-e-e-e:

come leaping towards you for a moment, white curls,
their mother,
urinating in the sodden field,
silent.

Ah,
the Great White Sheep
(this line a great white silence –
now a traffic hindrance
and some cause for poetry at easter-time

yesterday
I saw Shona
and she asked, in the home-coming
what this flower was, and that:

lily-of-the-valley, she said,
and primrose and forget-me-not and buttercup

and finally I danced a ballet with her,

da-ra-da-da-da-da-da-da
da-ra-da-da-da-da-da-da-da
da-ra-da-da (slow down) da-da
(now faster) da-ra-da-da-da-da-da-da-da-da-da-da-da-da

and the world spinning

in smiles

I am a rose
I am a rose of Sharon
a lily, a lily, a lily, a lily, a lily

of the glen:

All beautiful you are, my darling:
    there is no flaw in you (Song of Songs: 4:7).

The Sound of a Hammer

A complete lifetime has almost destroyed me,
but I hear the sound of a hammer
telling me that you loved me so, so much

Daddy

this sound on wood is your beautiful brow
sweating
and the house we stayed in, the hut, alive with children
hammering

this moment is complete silence
except the sound of hammer on wood

except the sound of hammer on wood
this moment is complete silence

and see, how the sweet shavings curled down from the sharp plane,
how the sweet shavings curled down from the sharp plane:

tonight the electric fire makes a soft, warm noise

but then, then there was the sound of a hammer on wood.

Eating Scones

This was the High Summer of the Prince's Pride:
by July,
he was declaring his father King in the capital, Edinburgh –
Carlisle fell, followed by Penrith and Manchester and Derby:
by the time he reached Swarkstone Bridge,
London (so the script says), was in chaos

until his decent general, Lord George Murray,
said "go home".

The end came on a cold day
when my people were slaughtered by ambition, greed and lies.

He spent many years
dying,
soaked in wine and sad venereal disease.

Beinn a' Choraraidh and the Prince's cave,
where the heather really is blue in Spring,
I remember Easter mornings when I was a child
and the sun dancing astonishingly to the north above Ben Mòr
as we went to Holy Communion in white, white, shirts and a shadow-flash of tartan.

My first love, there are many pictures for your choosing,
but these days everything is very beautiful,
eating scones in Katie's kitchen.

Bus Journey

I can imagine her –
though imagine is the wrong word –
remembering all of us by name:
as how we were, blonde and newly home from school

the car lights sweeping all ways now

this day my daughter my daughter
your picture sits upon my table,
your hands outstretched, my mother pouring forth

when I remember every tittle of the day,
boys in Kyle, contraceptives, cheesecake,

I remember my mother,
awake in an empty house
and those young, proud, girls on the bus,
talking like adults in a new, shocking, world.

In The Sink

I hear my mother at the sink
knowing that she is no poem, but that Marx was right:
we have all been robbed of our humanity.

Seagulls
are my constant companions,
wheeling, then standing on seaweedy outcrops
pecking at something quite invisible.

Without
casting any great lines into history,
here I am, washing dishes in the sink,
like my mother and father, like every Chrissie.

Even though there is a loved landscape here that I well know:
firewood from last year's barbecue,
someone else's wall,
and then the inevitable great sea, the seagulls' specific environment.

Beyond,
(even in the haze), lies the flat lands of Uist:
all machair, all cattle, all armaments,
claimed, though I never yielded it, by a new generation.

Beyond that, they say, lies the universe of the whole world:
Derek Walcott,
Jerusalem,
and the exploited history of everyone in the whole world.

The universe is filled with great stories
that have, finally, filtered down to this sink:
my mother stands, grey and bowed,
an Gàidheal air a mhilleadh, gun tilleadh, gun tilleadh.

"Say Something In Gaelic, Mister"

And this was in Portree:
6 year old kid,
and his grandfather, cottar from Bracadale,
drowned on the 'Hercules', Vatersay forgotten

my beautiful daughter,
where no grandfather reigns, there was tuberculosis, typhoid and cholera:
amidst the bonny sighs

remember Portree this day
and that child,
asking.

Mingulay

This,

is where we wanted

to get

married.

Here,

in the white cup

of Mingulay.

Sand,

covering the ancient hearth-stones.

Blàbheinn

Ciamar
nach urrainn dhomh do chur am briathran
mo ghaol as àirde

ach dìreach   Blàbheinn
blàth a' bheinn
blàth a' bheinn a-nochd
's mi sìnt air do ghuailnean geal' àlainn
socair

snaidhm do ghuailne
a' choire shuainich, choire shuainich, choire shuainich,
corranach corranach corranach

darabadì darabadì darabadì o hi-hò
darabadì darabadì darabadì o hi-hò
darabadì darabadì darabadì o hi-hò
darabadì darabadì darabadì o hi-hò
darabadì darabadì darabadì o hi-hò

aisling
do chraiceann mìn, do chraiceann mìn, do chraiceann mìn o hi-hò
do bhilean ròs, do bhilean ròs, do bhilean ròs o hi-hò

faclan nèimh, faclan nèimh, faclan nèimh o hi-hò
faclan sèimh, faclan sèimh, faclan sèimh, o hi-hò
faclan naomh, faclan naomh, faclan naomh, o hi-hò
faclan caomh, faclan caomh, faclan naomh o hi-hò

faclan gaoil, faclan gaoil, faclan gaoil o hi-hò
gnìomhan gaoil, gnìomhan gaoil, gnìomhan gaoil o hi-hò

Blàbheinn

How
can I not put you into words
my highest love

except to say   Blàbheinn
warm/blossoming the mountain
warm/blossoming the mountain tonight
and I stretched on your beautiful white shoulders
in the stillness

the grip of your shoulders
sleepy corries, sleepy corries, sleepy corries
corranach corranach corranach

darabadì darabadì darabadì o hi-hò
darabadì darabadì darabadì o hi-hò
darabadì darabadì darabadì o hi-hò
darabadì darabadì darabadì o hi-hò
darabadì darabadì darabadì o hi-hò

dream
skin smooth, skin smooth, skin smooth o hi-hò
lips red, lips red, lips red o hi-hò

words heavenly, words heavenly, words heavenly o hi-hò
words quiet, words quiet, words quiet o hi-hò
words holy, words holy, words holy o hi-hò
words gentle, words gentle, words gentle o hi-hò

words of love, words of love, words of love o hi-hò
deeds of love, deeds of love, deeds of love o hi-hò

Ciamar
nach urrainn dhomh do chur am briathran
mo ghaol as airde

ach dìreach   Blàbheinn
blàth a' bheinn
blàth a' bheinn a-nochd
's mi sìnt' air do ghuailnean geal' àlainn
socair

snaidhm do ghuailne
a' choire shuainich, choire shuainich, choire shuainich,
corranach corranach corranach

darabadì darabadì darabadì o hi-hò
darabadì darabadì darabadì o hi-hò
darabadì darabadì darabadì o hi-hò
darabadì darabadì darabadì o hi-hò
darabadì darabadì darabadì o hi-hò

How
can I not put you into words
my highest love

except to say   Blàbheinn
warm/blossoming the mountain
warm/blossoming the mountain tonight
and I stretched on your beautiful white shoulders
in the stillness

the grip of your shoulders
sleepy corries, sleepy corries, sleepy corries,
corranach corranach corranach

darabadì darabadì darabadì o hi-hò
darabadì darabadì darabadì o hi-hò
darabadì darabadì darabadì o hi-hò
darabadì darabadì darabadì o hi-hò
darabadì darabadì darabadì o hi-hò

21

Sgalaraidh

Boireannach mòr
cruinn ann an dòigh Ghaidhealach:
làidir, seasgar, foghaineach.

Na fir
aig muir.

Saoghal nam brataichean dathach agus
saoghal nam ban,
clèibh air dromannan leathann.

Sgalaraidh

A big woman,
rounded in a Gaelic way:
strong, secure, well-becoming.

The men
at sea.

The world of coloured flags and
the world of the women,
creels on wide backs.

Dàn an t-Sabhail

Ann an dòigh, 's e carragh-chuimhne dha na fuadaidhean a
th' ann an Sabhal Mòr Ostaig, air a thogail dhan tuathanas
mhòr fhad 's a bha na daoine fhèin air an clìoradh: ach tha
dà latha air tighinn.

Nach iomadh oileanach
nach fhaca riamh leabhar no colaisde
ach dìreach trèisgeir, locair agus bochdainn
a chaidh a thilgeil a-null a Chanada:
"village Hampdens" theirear riutha anns a' chànan fhuar
nach d'fhuair ach fògradh, cianalas agus bàs:
tha an ceumanachadh anns an fheur, anns an arbhar, anns an èadhar:
na daoine bochda nach fhaca colaisde riamh
beò len òrain agus len ùrnaighean
nam chuimhne, nam chogais, nam fhuil, nam chnàmhan, nam cheann, nam bhàrdachd:
an sabhal airson nam beathaichean, 's Canada airson nan daoine –
cuireamaid sin sna coimpiutairean 's deànamaid hì-ho-ro-hiù dheth.

Dàn an t-Sabhail (The Song of the Barn)

In a way, Sabhal Mòr Ostaig (The Big Barn of Ostaig), the Gaelic College
on Skye, stands as a memorial to the Highland Clearances, having
originally been built as a barn for the large farm whilst the people
themselves were being cleared: but, perhaps, times have changed.

The many students
who never saw either a book or college
but peat-ploughs, wood-planes and poverty,
who were flung across to Canada:
"village Hampdens" they were called in the cold language,
who received nothing but exile, homesickness and death:
their graduation is in the rocks of the Highlands,
their education in the hay, in the corn, in the air:
the oppressed people who never saw a college
alive with their songs and prayers
in my memory, in my conscience, in my blood, in my head, in my poetry:
the Sabhal (barn) for the animals, and Canada for the people –
let's feed that into the computers and make a hì-ho-ro-hiù (a song-and-dance) of it.

In The Middle of the Street

The stars were in place.

Orion, once more, over the Greek Mountain.

Venus.

You, you, over the generous Cuillin,

And (if truth be told), we were afraid.

The peat road
runs between my father and my father,
where, on days when the rocks glistened
we drank corked milk
and the hairs on his arms, wisps of cloudburst over Eiseabhal,
shone

and beyond,
Eoghainn Phàdraig, Eoghainn Phàdraig (It's no cold here, it's cold on the lakes)
rested,
and Eàirdsidh Beag and Dòmhnall Sheumais and Iagan and Dòmhnall Uilleim and
Peigi Mhòr,

in the middle of the peat road,
here in Pilton,
his mother cries "WULL-YAM"

and I don't love him enough fur his ginger name.

At Your Granny's

Now take your Granny, fae Dundee:
on Saturdays, after Doctor Who,
giving you egg and chips, and a thick slice of half-loaf.

Then home, counting the Christmas trees on the way.

Counting The Christmas Trees

A cold coming we had of it,
and such a time for a journey:
after ice-skating, and there was one, and two, and three
and a hundred, glittering, all over Edinburgh.

Let's make it 1969
and the horses coughing down at Tollcross
on one of the last milk journeys.
(I have a picture of you, aged 9, in your tutu in the back garden.)
It's getting dark,
and the dead are already hallucinating up in the Grassmarket.
Men are celebrating Hibs' victory,
and women, as ever, are doing the shopping.

There's one,
and two,
and three,
and another, and another and another and another, all glittering.

The Cameo is lit up, and the Caledonian,
and lovers rush into the Waverley.

On the Island of Seil, I stand, combing my hair.
Darling Darling : you and you.

Let's make it 1939
and the horses coughing down at Tollcross
on one of the last milk journeys.
(I have a picture of you, aged 9, in your kilt in the back garden.)
It's getting dark,
and the dead are already hallucinating up in the Grassmarket.

After such a cold coming, after such a journey.
Men are celebrating Hibs' victory,
and women, as ever, are doing the shopping.

There's one,
and two,
and three,
and another, and another and another and another, all glittering.

The Cameo is lit up, and the Caledonian,
and lovers rush into the Waverly.

All this was before the blitz.

Let's make it 1919
and the horses coughing down at Tollcross
on one of the last milk journeys.
(I have no photograph of my father, aged 9 at that time.)
It's getting dark,
and the dead are already hallucinating up in the Grassmarket.
After such a cold coming, after such a journey.
Men are celebrating Hibs' victory,
and women, as ever, are doing the shopping.

There's one,
and two,
and three,
and another, and another and another and another, all glittering.

The Cameo is lit up, and the Caledonian,
and lovers rush into the Waverley.

Then at dawn we came down to a temperate valley,

Wet, below the snow line, smelling of vegetation;
With a running stream and a water-mill beating the darkness,
And three trees on the low sky.

And the horses coughing down at Tollcross
on one of the last milk journeys.

I have a picture of you.

Let's make it 1991,
after ice-skating, and there was one, and two, and three
and a hundred, all glittering.

Miss Beth White

At nine years of age
it is wonderful
to be called

Miss.

The postcards are by the Medici Society Ltd,
this particular one
The Twighlight Dance by Molly Brett.

Other cards, for Master David, make the world rougher:
it is all rabbits and seals and otters and badgers.

The text, in beautiful rounded English
(how this woman loves these children)
speaks of sun and sea and sand and summer.

And praise be for the Post Office
whose constantly smudged dates
make these cards permanently innocent.

Sharon Templeman

This thin girl in Pilton
with five straggling children
has named them, each in turn :
I hear 'Sharon' and 'Kylie' and 'Jason' and 'Ewen' and 'Robbie',
their individual names bitten out in anger and despair.

Thatcher's Children have been left with nothing to name.

I write, pretty comfortably,
here in Skye,
where I can name the Cuillin Ridge out the picture-window :
Gàrs Bheinn, Sgurr nan Eag, Sgurr Dubh Mòr, Sgurr Alasdair and on and on,
as if they mattered, really mattered.

Gaelic is not spoken any more.

The first time
ever I saw your face
I thought the sun rose in your eyes
and I named you Elizabeth, Queen of England,
Dei Regina, Fidei Def, the everlasting coin.

I want to swallow the sea, because there's so much of it.

One look at the Ordnance Survey
tells me that other things mattered to Sharon :
Cnoc na Fuarachd, Teampuill Chaoinn, Coill' a' Ghasgain,
Daliburgh, Bathgate, Kilmarnock,
and the green green burial places of Larkin's England.

The Quaker Graveyard in Nantucket for your cousin, Nina.

Have the dead been robbed?
Their thin fingers left without rings,
the gold and the braids gone,
the simple brass plates removed,
everything – everything but the hard bones – stolen.

Them bones, them bones, them dry bones.

Scotland,
you desecrated universe
with gaunt, dying eyes.
Sharon Templeman, do you have a penny,
a child, you can name?

I live in Number 25.

One road.

A silver wheel.

A flash of red.

A flash of blue.

Czechoslovakia.

Me.

And you.

Gearradh na Mònadh à Smeircleit

Taigh Fhionnlaigh,
Taigh a' Bhaoghlaich,
Taigh Aonghais a' Cheanadaich,
Taigh Aonghais 'ac Dhòmhnaill,
Taigh Alasdair Ruaidh,
Taigh an Ruaidh,
Taigh Dhòmhnaill Eachainn,
Taigh Sheumais Shlàdair,
Taigh a' Chlachair,
Taigh Sheonaidh Mhòir,
Taigh Alasdair Dhuibh,
Taigh Phàdraig Eoghainn,
Taigh Sheonaidh Ailein,
Taigh Dhòmhnaill Penny,
Taigh Iagain Dhòmhnaill.

Mar a bha,
's mar a tha,
's mar a bhitheas.

Fad saoghal nan saoghal.

Amen.

Garrynamonie from Smerclate

Finlay's house,
The Benbecula man's house,
Angus, son of the Kennedy's, house,
Angus MacDonald's house,
Red Alasdair's house,
Domhachann's house,
A Ruaidh's house,
Donald Hector's house,
Seumas Shladair's house,
George's house,
The Stonemason's house,
Big Johnny's house,
Black Alasdair's house,
Patrick Ewen's house,
Seonaidh Allan's house,
Donald son of Penny's house,
Iagan Dhomhnaill's house.

As it was,
is,
and will be.

World without end.

Amen.

Names At The Swimming Pool

Driving champions who may be dead now.

Dates, achievements, split-second winners.

Some heroes winning five, six, seven, years in a row.

Later,
they went to university in these long coats
and became me.

One,
Elaine MacKenzie, breast stroke winner of 1972,
works in the florist in Academy Street.

That's all I know.

The final name is
Brenda Sherrat,
the first woman to swim Loch Ness.

31 hours, 27 minutes.

And her coach was Tom Pocklington of Solihull.

Can we go now, please, Dad?

South Lochboisdale

Here is another place where we have all been :
down past the vet's house,
down past the old teachers' house,
down on to the great, flat, stretch of rocks
where we waited, in the sunset, for the ferry.

I told you that the seals would surface to a Gaelic song
and you asked, my darling, that I would sing
an ancient crùnluath that would entice the entire universe.

There's a popular song, 'Eilidh',
with no ancient lyric and no great music,
and I sang it, loudly, unashamedly,
until the seals surfaced.

Then the ferry itself came round the far point
into the great, distant, port of Loch Boisdale.

A Liondsaidh, a ghràidh.

Walking The Single-Track Road

Is now an extraordinary experience,

as if
Mor Bhròdaidh, Seumas Shlàdair and Seumas Dhùghaill

never existed.

This road,
empty as it is, being mid-winter,
leads from Ord to Tarscabhaig, O my love.

When you walked inland
first of all there was the football pitch on the left
then the heap of stones leading to the curved right, and the houses beyond.

This is what Jim Hunter wrote:
"... The black house of a century or so ago was a grim and
unprepossessing dwelling. Its wall were perpetually damp. It had no windows
and no chimney, the smoke from the fire which burned perpetually in one corner
being left to find its way out through a hole in the roof. The floor was
trampled mud; the furniture virtually non-existant. The crofter's cattle
lived under the same straw-thatched, leaking roof as the crofter and his
family. Beasts and humans entered by the same door. In these dark, dank,
insanitary and foul-smelling homes, typhoid and cholera persisted long after
they had been eradicated in many other parts of Britain. And that most
dreaded of island disease, tuberculosis, haunted the black house well into
the present century."

Here,
where half the houses on this beautiful road
are holiday homes

I burn with anger
that the people are all dead.

Angus James MacDonald

Yesterday,

I caught someone like him

out of the corner of my eye.

In oilskins,

they did mysterious things

in barns, on wet Sunday afternoons.

Necessary things

such as carting dung.

Like reading Richard Hugo's great, great poem:

> Lord, it took no more than the wave of a glove,
> a nod of the head over tea. People were torn from their crofts
> and herded abroad, their land turned over to sheep.
> They sailed, they wept.
> The sea said nothing and said I'll get even.
> Their last look at Skye lasted one hour. Then fog.
> Think of their fear. When you can't read, not even a map,
> where does home end and Tasmania start?
> Think of the loss that goes stormy knots beyond bitter
> and think of some absentee landlord home in his tower
> signing the order and waving off a third ale.

Want an equation? O.K. The lovelier the land
the worse the dispossession, I know that's not right.
Blacks weep when put out of a shack,
Puerto Ricans to see the slum torn down.
We've all lost something or we're too young to lie,
to say we hear crofters sobbing
every high tide, every ferry that sails
Uig for Lewis, that vague shape out there in the haze.
We don't hear them sob. We don't know that they did.
And that form in the haze might be nothing,
not a destination, no real promise of home.

Some afternoons when pressure builds in the bay
and I think the sea will explode one more
mile per hour of gale, I wave my hand
and have the ship abort. I bring them back
and say it was a mistake. The landlord was drunk.
He's happy you're here. Don't worry. I'll find room
for the sheep. They laugh hard as money
and sing back to their crofts. When water relaxes
into a lazy roll home, Lewis stark in clear air,
I know they'd come ashore the way they left,
numbed by hard labour and grime
and I'd be no friend in their flat eyes.

Sons and Fathers

"Your sons will take the place of your fathers;" : Psalm 45:16a

All of a sudden,
only one of my father's generation is left alive,
ill and suffering.

And it – almost – made me cry.

Daughter,
daughter in a new-strange world,
they were strong, really strong.

I saw it, saw it for myself in those immortal days.

What hope, over a cup of tea.

What strength in a shovel.

What life in those beautiful Campbell veins.

I am completely devoid of words, despite my million poems.

And statements of faith sometimes come too easy:
With the Lord a day is like a thousand years,
and a thousand years are like a day.

I sit here today wanting it to be – for you – then, now.

It is 4.55.pm.

Blàbheinn is now my Biblical environment,
my Gilead, my Mount Hermon, my Mount Sinai,
my NIV cover.

41

It was July, and we sat in the kitchen
between shifts: there was soup and meat and rice
and many children tugging at our trouser legs.

I ate too fast, Bridget.

My darling, if you really study my face
you will see him there, swarthy and rounded and happy,
so very, very happy.

But listen, O daughter, consider and give ear:
Forget your people and your father's house.
The king is enthralled by your beauty;
honour him; for he is your lord.

Jonathan's Children

Don't forget, Angus Peter,
that there were others who were rock,
a Bethlehem of the heart.

(But you, Bethelehem Ephrathah,
though you are small among the
        clans of Judah,
out of you will come from me
        one who will be ruler over Israel,
whose origins are old,
        from ancient times.)

who lived in Judah, in Samaria, in Philistia, even in Israel itself.

Originally,
I see him as a small boy
threshing the waves in wonder –
when you stand in the water your feet get wet
he says with that marvellous little lisp that made everything innocent.

WHOOOOOOOOSH!
WHOOOOOOOOSH!
WHOOOOOOOOSH!
and the quiet fish-filled sea before them.

WE HAVE DESTROYED THAT INNOCENT SEA WITH OUR SINFUL GREED

Sarah,
Sarah, my beloved child
guard that threshing ocean with every lisp you can recall,
from the first tiny trinkle of bathing water until the last great apocolyptic storm.

Eòin

Rounded,
you begin life's voyage.

Somewhere,
where God breathed life into the very dust,

you were linked with a moment, a woman, a page, a poem.

I Love You

is the bird that has just taken off,

your high heels spicing behind me,

the black mantilla and the shawl,

the auburn hair and the drawn lines
spelling out 51 Glendales this new summer-time.

Your Photograph

there you are,
butterfly.

Once,
when I was really young –
about your age –
a butterfly hovered before my eyes
and I thought the world was entirely blue,
with the sea washing in between my toes,

and now you are here.

The imperfect will disappear,
as we smile, here,
watching the frail butterfly hover
between our outstretched hands
and the green, curling, leaves.

At the Peats in Boisdale

Bluebottles.

Nibbles.

On my bicycle, I surveyed whether it was a good or a bad day.

I could see him bending in the distance,
completely approachable.

Eòghainn Chailein in his overalls,
and it was worth – completely worth –
leaving the bike spinning in the short grass.

Saturday Afternoon

It's hard to believe now
that they went to confession
every Saturday afternoon

walking.

Peigi Chailein after the semolina,

Peigi Fhionnlaigh after the churning,

Peigi Iain Bharraich after the black cattle, herded.

I remember their poor black shoes
and the summer sun shining on their crouched backs
as I pumped up the football for another game after another.

Indians Dispossessed

'In the 1860s the U.S. government began confining Indians to reservations on less desirable lands.' : Note on National Geographic Society map.

In the very year
that my great-grandfather
was turfed-out by the whip-hand of the MacDonalds

(take your pick from Boreraig, Suishinish or South Uist)

the Indians (sometimes called Native Americans)
were being turfed-out by the same whip-hand.

(Take your pick between today's San Francisco and Florida.)

Here in Ord,
on a June June morning
I read the amazing names on this historic map:
Cheynee, Comanche, Crow, Arapaho, Soshone, Apache, Sioux
that I only knew from cowboy-and-indian films
in flickering Daliburgh (St Peter's) Hall.

And the expected illustrations:
their arms clenched across their great chests
like my grand-aunt's the day she died,
lying in that coffin in Smerclate.

I've just been re-reading The Croft History of South Uist
and there they are on the Great Northern Plains:
my great-great-great grandfather,
my great-great grandfather,
my great grandfather
and my grandfather (all on my mother's side) :

49

Alexander MacDonald, Angus MacDonald, Donald MacDonald and Ewen MacDonald,
their Indian genealogy rattling out at me in Gaelic:
Alasdair Raonuill,
Aonghas mac Alasdair Raonuill,
Dòmhnall mac Aonghais Alasdair Raonuill
agus Eòghainn mac Dhòmhnaill Aonghais Alasdair Raonuill, my mother's father.

The dispossession of the Great Tribes
is a scandal to my heart
when I hear the word freedom on American lips
and the 7th Cavalry decimated at the Little Bighorn.

(It made me weep terribly yesterday
to discover that Custer's poor widow, Elizabeth,
lived until 1933, the year my father was 23 with the whole world before him.)

I want to run,
even as Elisha did,
(with my cloak tucked into my belt)
down the villages Bornish and Stilligarry and Peninirene
and Dunfermline and Bolton and Penrith
and Pocatello and Denver and Pueblo
with the 41 sheets of Red Horse's pencil drawings:
can you see them.

Those stick figures, turned over,
one dead after another.

The commentary reads that at the time of the attack
the artist was digging wild turnips.

St Mirren 3 Aberdeen 1

The date: 25 April 1959.
(I've checked!)

We stand outside
Taigh Dhòmhnaill Chorodail
(I remember),
as Bryceland, Miller, Baker and Baird scored.
(I phoned the S.F.A. this morning and they told me.)

The wireless was in the window,
and at half-time we replayed the game
on the nearest patch of green, rocky grass.
(I recently saw how small, how very small, the patch was.)

The sun was shining, as it is today.

And the name Ian Ure,
that I've carried in my head
every moment of all my great pain
all these great, ridiculous, years.

A Field Guide in Colour to Birds, by Dr Walter Cerny

The Red-Breasted Flycatcher's song:
a slow, glissando 'tink-tink-tink-eida-eida-eida-hwee-da-hwee-da',
reminiscent of the song of the Willow Warbler.

The Lapwing (Vanellus vanellus):
size of pigeon, easily recognised by opalescent sheen
on black-green doral plumage and erectile, pointed crest.

The Short-Eared Owl:
Irregular, infrequent nester in wet, open country,
e.g. moors, wet meadows. When migrating,
appears in parties in potato fields, willow beds etc.

Hawfinch:
Diet: cherry-,sloe-,plum-stones, apple pips,
hard seeds of various decidious trees, insects.
Resident and nomadic bird.

Wood Warbler:
song composed of series of 'stip' notes repeated at same pitch,
with increasing rapidity, to
'stip, stip, stip, stip-stip-stip-stip- shreeeee'.
Often sung during fluttering display flight
introduced by fluty 'piu-piu-piu'.

Starling:
Nest: made of grass, straw, twigs, and feathers
in hole in tree or wall or nesting box.

Yellowhammer:
Eggs: 4-5, whitish, with brown spots and scribbles,

incubated 12-14 days (and young fed same duration)
by both parents.

The Fan-Tailed Warbler's song:
'cheek-tew-dzeep-dzeep'.

The Rock Bunting's song:
'zi-zi-zi-zirr'.

The Firecrest's song:
'zeezeezeezeezeezia'.

The Chiffchaff's song:
'chiff, chaff, chiff, chaff'.

The Greenfinch's song:
'chichichichit-tswerrr-tru-teu-teu-chup-chupchup-djul-djul-djul'.

The Wood Lark's song:
'lu-lu-lu-lu-lu', 'toolooeet toolooeet toolooeet'.

darabadì darabadì darabadì o hi-hò
darabadì darabadì darabadì o hi-hò
darabadì darabadì darabadì o hi-hò
darabadì darabadì darabadì o hi-hò
darabadì darabadì darabadì o hi-hò

tink-tink-tink-eida-eida-eida-hwee-da-hwee-da
size of pigeon easily recognized by opalescent sheen
e.g. moors, wet meadows. When migrating,
Diet: cherry-, sloe-, plum-stones, apple pips
stip, stip, stip, stip-stip-stip-stip- shreeeee
in hole in tree or wall or nesting box

incubated 12-14 days (and young fed same duration)

cheek-tew-dzeep-dzeep

zi-zi-zi-zirr

teek-teet-tai-tississik

zeezeezeezeezeezia

chiff, chaff, chiff, chaff

chichichichit-tsweerrr-teu-teu-teu-chup-chupchup-djul-djul-djul-djul

lu-lu-lu-lulu-lu, toolooeet toolooeet toolooeet

darabadî darabadî darabadî o hi ·hò.

Another Bird Song

Before me lies Loch Eishort in all its bare beauty.

Sea.

Rocks.

Waves.

One small blue boat.

Rain.

Mist.

And grey sky.

The ultimate in all-round vision is seen in the woodcock where the eyes are placed high on the head and well to the back, giving it a full 360 visual field. It can therefore see all round itself, including directly behind, and it is impossible for anyone or anything to approach it unobserved.

Hear these words:
It can see all round itself, including directly behind.

Incredible!

Just like God,
Birds are very beautiful, and mean everything to me.

Do you remember, dear brother,

the plovers' nests curled in the grey grass,
the four spotted eggs like four extraordinary universes?

And that day the insects crept on to the water-lilies?

And that day we heard the sparrow in Eoghainn Phàdraig's chimney?

And the day we sailed through the Sound of Eriskay?

And the day the porpoises almost swamped
me and my Dad and 'Illesbuig Neill.

And the day we fished at the pier-head.

But the facts,
at least as far as we know them,
continue.

There are about 9,000 species of living birds.

The American Golden Plover migrates, annually, a distance of 22,000 miles.

The Albatross beats its wings once in every half an hour.

The tiny Humming Bird beats its wings 200 times a second.

Incredible!

Staring ahead,
my vision is parametered by the Aird of Sleat and Strathaird.
The clearest thing
is a group of five houses over at Glas na Cille,
though they are too far away (and the day too grey)

to make out very clearly.

A TV Mast stands like an ancient monument on the horizon.

Four birds (cormorants) have just taken wing.

Waves.

Seventeen (as far as I can count) fishing bouys.

Then something horrible from that beautiful book on birds:
"Feathers", it says, "evolved from reptilian scales".

Just imagine!

The awfulness of it all.

Do you remember, in Wisconsin,
that bird we watched, flying west,
its wings glinting in the sunset?

And James, bonny James MacLeod of Idaho,
do you remember the day we watched the huge whooper swans
gulfing down the Sound of Raasay? Wasn't it wonderful?

Bird ancestry, it says, can be traced back to the reptiles, and fossil
evidence indicates that birds evolved in the Jurassic Period about 180
million years ago. Archaeopteryx is regarded as one of the first birds and
it possessed many characterisitcs, such as a long bony tail, peg-like teeth
and three claws on each wing, alongside the obvious bird characteristics.

On your finger is the engagement ring I gave you,
two birds locked in flight.

A few other scattered memories:
the seagulls eating our fish-and-chips,
the first redbreast of that first winter,
the bird-songs when you were in bed, in bed ill, as a child.

The warmth, the warmth, of the great, great back.

The bird-songs of Edinburgh,
reluctance fading in the chichichlchil-tsweerrrr teu-teu-teu-chupchup.

A sentimental line from me:
the morning light of love.

Here is the final, dreadful paragraph of the book:

As members of the mammalian class we might not care to be reminded that
the mammals are in decline like many other animal groups before them. In
the world today there are approximately 4,500 species of mammals, whereas
birds number approximately 8,6000 species, insects 700,000 species and even
the Protozoa number about 30,000 species (see the Handbook of British
Mammals by H.N. Southern). However, it must also be remembered that one
species of mammal, Homo sapiens (man), is rapidly increasing in number
and over the last million years has made a tremendous impact upon the world.

On the radio this morning
a woman said that because evolution had now ceased
we were now no longer biological, but cutural, creatures.

Before me lies Loch Eishort in all its bare beauty.

Love Sequence

1.

Worlds apart: you in your small corner
and I in mine.

You walked abroad
in a shower of all my days.

Strangers,
strangers in the night, exchanging glances.

My love.

11.

Names, near places, distant places: Benbecula.

That night, the round edge of a table.

Yes,
possibly.

111.

Praise Him.

Praise Him in the morning.

Praise Him.

Praise Him in the noontime.

Praise Him.

Praise Him when the sun goes dow-ow-own.

Praise Him.

IV.

China's.

That walk, that walk, that walk.

The promise that I love you.

V.

Chug-a-chug a chug-a-chug
a chug-a-chug a chug-a-chug
chug-a-chug a chug-a-chug
a chug-a-chug a chug-a-chug
a-chug.

VI.

This morning, the sea surges on to the shore
right in front of my house, right in front of my eyes.

Here,

at this very table.

VII.

O mosglamaid gu suilbir ait
le sunndach gasd' is eireamaid ...

VIII.

A million, a million momentos.

At the corner of the street.

Your smile in prayer.

IX.

O great Island, Island of my love,
many a night of them I fancied
the great ocean itself restless
agitated with love of you
as you lay on the sea,
great beautiful bird of Scotland.

X.

Your supremely beautiful wings bent
about many-nooked Loch Bracadale,
your beautiful wings prostate on the sea
from the Wild Stallion to the Aird of Sleat,
your joyous wings spread
about Loch Snizort and the world.

XI.

O Lyndsay, Lyndsay, my love
many a night I lay stretched
by your side in that slumber
when the mist of twilight swathed you.
My love every leaflet of heather on you
from Rudha Hunish to Loch Slapin,
and every leaflet of bog-myrtle kin
from Stron Bhiornaill to the Garsven,
every tarn stream and burn a joy

61

from Romisdale to Brae Eynort,
and even if I came in sight of Paradise,
what price its moon without Blàbheinn?

XII.

Ciamar
nach urrainn dhomh do chuir am briathran
mo ghaol as àirde
ach dìreach   Blàbheinn
blàth a'bheinn
blàth a' bheinn a-nochd
's mi sìnt air do ghuailnean geal' alainn
socair

snaidhm do ghuailne, a Liondsaidh,
a' choire shuainich, choire shuainich, choire shuainich,
corranach corranach corranach

darabadì darabadì darabadì o hi-hò
darabadì darabadì darabadì o hi-hò
darabadì darabadì darabadì o hi-hò
darabadì darabadì darabadì o hi-hò
darabadì darabadì darabadì o hi-hò

aisling
do chraiceann mìn, do chraiceann mì, do chraiceann mìn o hi-hò
do bhilean ròs, do bhilean ròs, do bhilean ròs o hi-hò

faclan nèimh, faclan nèimh, faclan nèimh o hi-hò
faclan sèimh, faclan sèimh, faclan sèimh o hi-hò

faclan naomh, faclan naomh, faclan naomh o hi-hò
faclan caomh, faclan caomh, faclan caomh o hi-hò

faclan gaoil, faclan gaoil, faclan gaoil o hi-hò
gnìomhan gaoil, gnìomhan gaoil, gnìomhan gaoil, o hi-hò

How
can I not put you into words
my highest love

except to say   Blàbheinn
warm/blossoming the mountain
warm/blossoming the mountain tonight
and I stretched on your beautiful white shoulders
in the stillness

the grip of your shoulders, Lyndsay,
sleepy corries, sleepy corries, sleepy corries,
corranach corranach corranach

darabadì darabadì darabadi o hi-hò
darabadì darabadì darabadi o hi-hò
darabadì darabadì darabadi o hi-hò
darabadì darabadì darabadi o hi-hò
darabadì darabadì darabadi o hi-hò
darabadì darabadì darabadi o hi-hò
darabadì darabadì darabadi o hi-hò
darabadì darabadì darabadi o hi-hò
darabadì darabadì darabadi o hi-hò
darabadì darabadì darabadi o hi-hò
darabadì darabadì darabadi o hi-hò
darabadì darabadì darabadi o hi-hò.

The People Of The Arctic, Themselves

Here they are, listed on the vast circled map:

The Chukchi

The Yakut

The Evenk

The Nenets

The Lapps

The West Greenlanders

The Polar

The Baffin Islanders

The Central Canadians

The Kutchin

The Aleut

The North Alaskans

The fur-skinned drawings emerge out of the petrochemical data.

Queen Flora the First

The phrase emerges like a memorial from my brain:
The Crusades.

And I see helmeted Knights, with sharp spears, being oh,
so valiant.

Richard the Lionheart, so very brave
and big and tall and strong and handsome
and the golden-haired maidens a-weeping
for him, and bringing his heart home, always in a silver casket,
to Canterbury.

They were valiant,
these sons of the soil:
no fifes or drums did bugle blow
when Peigi Dhòmhnaill Sheumais they laid her down, last week, in Hàllain Hill.

Da-daidh

Ged a bhiodh reacòrdair air a bhith ann
a' dearbhadh
gur e 'Dadaidh'
a' chiad fhacal,

dè 'n deifir?

Oir, seall –
na cnuic: Eiseabhal, a' Bheinn Mhòr agus Hecla.

Iain Dhòmhnaill Alasdair
Dùghall Alasdair Sheumais
Peigi Iain Bharraich

abidil nan aibidil:
Gleann Dail, Taobh a' Chaolais, Cille Bhrìghde, Smeircleit, Gearraidh na
Mònadh, An Leth Mheadhanach, Baghasdal, Taobh a Deas Loch Baghasdail,
An Sròm, Cille Pheadair, Dalabrog, Loch Baghasdail, Gearraidh
Sheilidhidh, Aisgeirnis.

A is for Apple
B airson Ball
C is for Carrot
D airson Dall

An aibidil Ghàidhlig, a Dhadaidh,
air a deanamh le m' eudail òg:

Da-ddy

Even if there had been a recorder
to verify
that 'Daddy'
was the first word

so what?

For, look –
the hills: Eiseabhal, Ben More and Hecla.

Iain Dhòmhnaill Alasdair
Dùghall Alasdair Sheumais
Peigi Iain Bharraich

alphabet of alphabets:
Glendale, East Kilbride, West Kilbride, Smerclate, Garrynamonie,
South Boisdale, North Boisdale, South Lochboisdale, Strome,
Kilpheder, Daliburgh, Lochboisdale, Garryhallie, Askernish.

A is for Apple
B is for Ball
C is for Carrot
D is for Blind

The Gaelic alphabet, Daddy,
composed by my young darling:

Horizon

A merchant navy ship on the horizon
between Rum and South Uist,
and we are all sixteen.

There are losses that go stormy beyond bitter knots,
never sailed
never sailed
never sailed

never taken, Christine.

A Dhòmhnaill Eòsaph, 'ille,
nach math g' eil thu beò
's a' seòladh nan cuantan

a dh'Astràilia-null.

stone upon stone

fine flower upon fine flower

machair upon machair: A Mhàiri bheag, cuimhnich do chuid Gàidhlig.

Today,
in that perpetual gap between Strathaird and the Aird of Sleat,
I'm sure I saw a ship, (a merchant navy ship),
stirring the horizon between Rum and South Uist.

God's carts overflow with abundance (Psalm 65:11b)

He trundles off,

up the hillside

on the South Boisdale peat-road

the curving cart loaded high, rickety, shoogling,
hitting stones, bumpity, and shallow, then deep, oily pools of water

almost sideways turning into the hill-gate

a safe plomp into the dry almost-grain and look

down there

He comes

the thick hay spilling over and He sitting – with a pipe, of all things –
puffing on the rusty cross-bar

waving at – who is it? – Eoghainn Chailein waving
back waving at me waving.

The Moon, Tonight

Is five billion years old
as I listened to the news
direct from around this globe:
a President has been assassinated,
a Prime Minister has shot himself,
and a football team has been relegated
from the globe this is the news this night, good night.

And the moon, this night,
has a face like a clock in the hall:
like when I was a child in South Boisdale
and I would stand looking up at it while I peed at the back door.
I can recall the arc of the urine
and its fizzy noise on the frosty grass, and the moon and the stars
and the eternal Catholic sky.
On returning I would perhaps hear
my father cough
and the light of the rushing moon spilling through the window
over Angus' curved figure, and Donald Joseph's curled hand,
and Margaret, and maybe Ann-Marie, sleeping next door,
and then lying, for those long moments
waiting to escape sleep, and you were gone

towards this moon this night
spilling through this window
on to the cough of my father's breath listening to me
returning from peeing, right there, at the back door.

Fidel Castro's Mother Sang

There, there, my darling boy,
there, there, my bairnie,
there, there, my darling child,
there, there, a' m'eudail.

The soldier men are on the hill,
they won't come a-near ye,
the soldier men are far awa',
rest, my bonnie dearie.

Fidel, Fidel, my bonnie dear,
sleep just now my dearie-o;
the sound of war is far awa',
rest, my bonnie dearie.

Hòbhan, hòbhan, Goiridh òg ò,
Goiridh òg ò, Goiridh òg ò;
Hòbhan, hòbhan, Goiridh òg ò,
gun d' fhalbh mo ghaol 's gun d'fhàg e mi.

Dh'fhàg mi 'n seo na shìneadh e,
na shìneadh e, na shìneadh e,
gun d'fhàg mi 'n seo na shìneadh e,
nuair dh'fhalbh mi bhuain nam braoileagan.

Fhuair mi lorg an dòbhrain duinn;
an dòbhrain duinn, an dòbhrain duinn;
fhuair mi lorg an dòbhrain duinn,
's cha d'fhuair mi lorg mo chaoineachain.

Fidel, Fidel, my bonnie dear,
my bonnie dear, my bonnie dear;
Fidel, Fidel, my bonnie dear,
rest tonight, my dearie-o.

71

Oswiecim-Brzezinka

'Poland ... mother and nurse of the youth and younglings of Scotland,
clothing, feeding and enriching them with the fatness of her best things':
William Lithgow, after travelling extensively throughout Poland in 1616.

Outside,
the Minch is a grey calm
and, silently, my mother washes dishes in the sink.
It is late April
and Scotland is at peace with herself, like a late, middle-aged, mother.

Here, I spurn wealth and fame and fortune:
I only seek the moment of the hydro-wire,
the buzzard on your arm, your smile,
and all of us watching the marvellous nickelodean.

There was a day
we had lunch with Louise Wardle,
and watched each others' hair
falling on to excited foreheads, softly, softly now.

There was a day
we fed donkeys with Janis and Claire and Lesley
running , all running,
between green clumps and each other.

There was a day
we drove through Glencoe,
and climbed Blàbheinn, and sat by the pool
the sun eternal on the short grass.

We have just returned, my love,

from Uist
where we sought Loch Sgiobort and Bagh Hartabhagh
through car windows,
the rain like a flood and we reached, by sodden foot
ruins that beseeched us to leave them, Mary and Peggy
how we still love you.

So we return,
and outside the Minch is a grey calm
as I try to think of Poland
and what it means.

It rhymed, of course, once with Shetland and Jutland and Finland
as it lay red on the cracking map,
folded between Achtung and Stalin, the big fat bastard.

We were told that there had been a war once –
a complicated one involving the Archduke Ferdinand
and Serbs and Bosnia and trenches and shells
and the Iolaire sinking in Stornoway harbour
and the floo'ers o' the forest aa' weed awa',
the floo'ers o' the forest aa' weed awa'.

A wonderful woman called Jessie Kesson taught me
that Polish men were like men from South Uist:
at the time of the cutting of the hay they courted
and men and women fell in love,
Naoise approaching Argyll, and Abraham and Sarah and Gràinne and Eimhir,
all of us standing before the marvellous nickelodean, hearing the great music.

On Flanders Field the poppies grow,
Between the crosses, row on row.

So that even the term Pollack became affectionate,
for on Sauchiehall Street I shared digs with that old Jew
who dipped his toast into his soft-boiled egg,
just like my grandfather.

And my uncle Donald was killed on a ship in the Clyde
while they were murdered, one after one after one
after one after one after one in vast graveyards
that would have swallowed all the Gaels of the last forty generations.

O, A Dhia
thoir mathanas dhomh airson Bosnia agus Croatia agus Serbia
agus gach leanabh gun ainm a tha falaichte 's an ainm Oswiecim,
air eader-theangachadh mar: Auschwitz.

Canaries

Now that you are here,
little bird ascended,

the less than mustard
seed of my tiny faith

permits me to trill a tiny note,
a minimal hallelujah: this poem.

I
hear
you
singing
upstairs

while the last evening mist
drifts west off the Cuillin
and the last seagull of the day descends, surely.

Ah, boys of Bahia Blanca,
girls of Kuala Lumpar,
remember tonight the last bell of the day:
the slow cattle coming here from the hills,
smokewood and languour on a summer's eve,
and the small boy, whistling, like a canary,
at the gloaming time that is you, now,
secure.

Pongo

was a fat man we used to know in Oban.

I called him Saturdays
for he carried odds-and-ends under his left arm (like Alf Tupper)
and reminded me of watching football on TV through electrical shop windows.

I actually wanted to use the word corpulent
because it seemed a more intelligent word.

But Pongo was a big fat man we used to know in Oban.

Pack

Pack the words tightly tightly into this new language
that would spin spurl rattle-out rattle-out great
great great love.

      I seek a new language for you
that would have nothing to do with Barra or Mingulay
or anywhere, anywhere at all that had anything at all
to do with anything at all:

I remember travelling on a train between Tangier and Casablanca
watching minstrels in white fielding in brown-red hedgerows,
inventing new words that are filled with grass-language,
Barren Brome, culms, oblong-lancelote.

Charles Edward Hubbard was born at Appleton, Norfolk, in 1900.
After intensive training in horticulture in the Royal Gardens,
Sandringham, and Oslo, Norway, and after serving in the RAF,
he entered the Royal Botanic Gardens, Kew, in 1920.

He became keenly interested in the large collection
of living plants for which Kew is world-renowned.

This interest led to his transference to the Herbarium in 1922
where he assisted the distinguished botanists of the famous Institution,
gaining general experience in the classification and identification
of flowering plants.

Since 1926 he has specialized in the study of grasses.

Pack the words tightly tightly into this new language
that would spin spurl rattle-out rattle-out great
great great love.

I seek a new language for you
that would have nothing to do with Barra or Mingulay
or anywhere, anywhere at all that had anything at all
to do with anything at all:

I remember travelling on a train between Tangier and Casablanca
watching minstrels in white fielding in brown-red hedgerows,
inventing new words that are filled with grass-language,
Barren Brome, culms, oblong-lancelote.

You were born somewhere, in the breath of God.

Tonight

A cascade of cards,
blu-tacked to the wall
stands out against the dark,
and a small cottage comes to mind
that I saw once, huddled against the South Uist shore.

It was winter, and all boarded up
and the sand cooried in against the wet walls
as the storm poured on to the soft felt roof.

That house deserved to have that night, as this,
a cascade of cards blu-tacked to the wall,
tilleys hissing against the storm.

Big Pencil

came on the bus at Ardfern

going to Lochgilphead for the Young Farmers' Ball.

He wore a tweed sports jacket

and drew a picture on the bus's breathy window

making a mark in the November night.

Now

Today, Blàbheinn looks like my father,
the first sprinkling of winter snow
and a tiny wisp of white cloud
brushing across his gentle forehead.

An Tràigh Siar

Chan e gu bheil glòir san taobh siar
no gu bheil sòlas anns na cuantan mòr

ach chunnaic mi thu

mar thrilleachan air an Tràigh Siar

cho aotrom le gàir' a Spioraid Naoimh.

The Western Strand

It's not that there is glory in the west
or that there is happiness in the great oceans

but I saw you

like sandpipers on the Western Strand

as free as the laughter of the Holy Ghost.

Chan E Cumha

(mar chuimhneachan air Donaidh Crotal)

Air an t-Sàbaid às deaghaidh do bhàis
tha na craobhan-beithe mar a bhà:
critheach, crùbach, lom,
a' greimeachadh ris a' bheinn.

Chan ann an seo
a dh'fhàsas craobhan mòra Chalifòrnia (gu nàdarra co-dhiù),
no craobhan-muncaidh Sheapan no fiù 's giuthas Nirribhidh:
chan eil an seo ach craobhan beaga Gaidhealach,
critheach, crùbach, lom,
a' greimeachadh ris a bheinn.

(The deagh fhios 'am gun deach coilltean mòr Alba
a sgriosadh o chionn lìnntean,
air an sgiùrsadh airson bàtaichean-cogaidh:
mo nàir oirnn, agus sinn fhathast a' losgadh san Amazon.)

Tha toiseach geamhraidh ann (ann an da-rìribh)
san dùthaich lom, ruadh, fhliuch is fhuar,
ach a-raoir chunna mi grunnan chaorach
a' gabhal fasgadh fo na croabhan critheach sa ghleann.

Sin agad samhla gun dean sinn an gnothach ri na th' ann.

84

Not An Elegy

(In memory of Donny Crotal)

On the Sabbath after your death
the birch-trees are as they were:
thin, hunched, bare, holding on to dear life on the mountainside.

It's not here
that the huge trees of California will grow (at least naturally),
or the monkey-trees of Japan or even the spruce of Norway:
here there are only elemental Highland trees,
thin, hunched, bare, holding on to the mountainside.

(I well know that the great woods of Scotland
were destroyed centuries ago,
uprooted in order to make war-ships:
shame on us, and us still burning the Amazon.)

It's the beginning of winter (nature's winter)
and the land is bare, brown, wet and cold,
but last night I saw a flock of sheep
taking shelter beneath the hunched trees in the glen.

That's a symbol that we'll make do with what we have.

I Used To Look In Ditches

I used to look in ditches for poetry:
frayed packets of Old Holburn,
plastic tubs of Numos Grease,
the occasional screwtop, bits of broken green glass, torn paper;

as if, when I was a child,
something meaningful could be found.

"Look" – you said to me one day –
"the texture of the sea – isn't it amazing?",
and for the first time, with you, I saw three-dimensional water.

When I was a child
we used to travel on the Claymore
and the best thing was standing on deck
waiting for he cook to throw cartons out the mess window:
how they sailed, these MacBrayne packets,
red and black and white, bobbing, towards Mull, until completely out of sight.

Lately I've taken to listening to the World Service.
Cricket scores, coups in Malawi, short stories from India,
and, as always, Cooke's letter from America.
Cartons chucked out the galley window.

I used to look in ditches for poetry:
frayed packets of Old Holburn,
plastic tubs of Numos Grease,
the occasional screwtop, bits of broken green glass, torn paper;

as if, when I was a child,
something meaningful could be found.

Willy Pastrano

was a boxer when I was wee.

I mumbled myself to sleep pronouncing his name
in my dreams.

Oh, Italian emigrants, how much pain.

He was a southpaw, leading with the right, jabbing,
catching them all off guard.

Willy Towill, Howard Winston, Floyd Paterson and I
winning, not with power, but with South Uist style.

Buth A' Bhaile

Bùth Ailein.

Bùth Dhòmhnaill Nealaidh.

Bùth Fhionnlaigh.

Bùth Ruaraidh Iain.

Eadar gach sgàineadh,
eadar an dealanach 's an tàirneanach,
bha sinn uile ri reic 's ri ceannach, ri reic 's ri ceannach,
oisglinean air feasgraichean geamhraidh, na sausages a' dol dheth as t-samhradh,
gus an tàinig am Free Press agus Am Pàipear agus an TV Times,
bollachan-mine ar làithean-ne.

Village Shop

Allan's shop.

Donald-Nelly's shop.

Finlay's shop.

Ruaraidh Iain's shop.

Between each split,
between the lightening and the thunder,
we were all at selling and buying, at selling and buying,
oilskins on winter afternoons, the sausages going-off in the summer,
till the Free Press, and the News of the Isles and the TV Times came,
the flour-sacks of our day.

Old Map of Jerusalem

Nowhere
could you find a more traditional city:
the Jebusite town captured by David, and extended and extended and extended.

Four roads,
like a distorted cross,
out of Jerusalem:
the ones to Bethlehem and Caesarea splitting like hairs at the Water Gate.

The map is coloured
pink for old blue for new and yellow for to be.

Out there,
in the yellow,
The Site of Calvary.

Elspeth Anderson

If death is to be heard
it is best heard here on Skye
at the time of the great evening silence
when the red hills lie blue between changing sea and sky

on this night above all
how appropriate that the great Minch rain sweeps against the window pane
from which hangs my orbed light, this table and the dresser
casting light against darkness

from which I close my eyes
to try and measure those things that were important:
the box of groceries you brought, and the electric blanket,
and the great hidden prayers raising me up into the presence of a God

in charge of dark as well as light,
Nepal as well as Granton, death as well as life:
if Cochabamba means anything, it is that only Christ remains, permanent,
when the red hill lies blue between changing sea and sky.

Dùn Deagh

A dh'aindeoin,
tha mi dol a'sgriobhadh mu ar deidhinn
ann an Gàidhlig:

gach uncail,
gach antaidh,
gach Tiomaidh,
gach Isa,

bonaidean air busaichean
seachad air Cill Rimhinn agus – seall – Queensferry (Aiseag na Bànrigh),

gus on do ràinig iad Gorgie
ann an teas-meadhan na Gàidhealtachd.

Dundee

Despite,
I am going to write about you
in Gaelic:

every uncle,
every auntie,
every Jimmy,
every Isa,

bonnets on buses
past St Andrews and – look – there's Queensferry (The Ferry of the Queen),

till they reached Gorgie
in the very heart of the Highlands.

Mr Sandy Eliot

"This is the car", he said.

"And this is the engine".

Pointing first to the car,

and, then, to the engine.

Here

I refuse to deal out images,
even ace after ace after ace.

I am easily tempted into love,
remembering tractors, and swans on the firth.

Last week, after two years' hesitation,
I ventured into Dunsgaith
where the pagan queen brewed fire-and-sword
in the easy bay round from my home.

Though I still fear her.

As a curtain against the full moon, I draw upon folk memories:
I think of hollowed hearth-stones, and a couple of my teachers,
and the first time we drove through Dollar, and the candles on this table –
perhaps anything will do.

At the bottom of the Brae of Trossaraidh
was the Mission House,
where the Protestants lived.

Baldo worked with the road-squad
and remembered ancient runes in his dreams.

Jonathon Wills was the student leader:
none, I'm told given to excessive drunkenness.

Most told lies or petty truths
because we had no idea what tomorrow held,
for I forgive you, I forgive you, I forgive you, Mr Major.

Now tonight is incredibly beautiful:
a purse-seiner is out in the bay,
its twin liturgies glittering, red and green.

There is no wind, no rain, no storm.

If I extinguished the lights and went outside,
I'm sure there would be stars.

Here,
where the rain has now begun,
I can hear your footsteps in the hall.

Faith holds me in.

The Abolition of Slavery

Christ,
says Scripture,
has abolished Death.

And the word abolished remains with me, like my child, clinging to my
breast.

I then remember the name William Wilberforce
and Garrynamonie School in the late fifties, when it always seemed to drizzle.

I also remember the headmaster in Oban
coming into Iain Crichton Smith's English class
and announcing that Mr Lobumba had died.

That evening, I discovered the meaning of the word assassinated.

And on that far South Uist day
I too was in bed
when news of Kennedy's death came through.

I think of accompanying my father in the ambulance to the hospital,
watching, outside, all that was so-familiar go swiftly by,
everything so immediately abolished.

Oidhche Chulaig

A-nochd chuimhnich mi air Oidhche Chullaig:
an t-àgh, an toileachas, an deasalachadh.

The mise nochd a' tighinn gur n-ionnsaigh
a dh'ùrachadh dhuibh na Cullaig;
cha ruig mi leas a bhith ga innse,
bha i ann ri linn mo sheanair.

'S a' chais ga cur mun cuairt,
's na faclan a' bruthadh a-mach:
silidh, ìm, càise, ("Mac Eòghainn Mhòir!") briosgaidean, is "stork" le gàire,

's suas, suas-suas gu Taigh Nill 'Illeasbaig
's na balaich aig taigh le òran is botal mòr,
fear le tastan, fear le leth-chrùn, fear leis a' "Chaiora".

Mo chaisean Cullaig ann am phòcaid,
's math an cèo thig às an fhear ud:
thèid e deiseil air na pàistean,
gu h-àraid air bean-an-taighe.

'S sìos, sìos seachad air an dìg,
's sìos, sìos seachad air an dìg,
(far am b' fheudar dhomh mùn),

mo chaisean Cullaig ann am phòcaid,
's math an cèo thig as an fhear ud.

'S cho doirbh 's a bha na faclan deireannach,
's tu cho beag (Cò aig a Dhia bha fios orra?).

Hogmany Night

Tonight I rememberd Hogmany night:
the anticipation, the joy, the preparation.

I am coming to-night to you
to renew for you Hogmanay;
I have no need to tell you of it,
it existed in the time of my grandfather.

And the skin-strip put round,
and the words pouring forth:
jam, butter, cheese, ("Big Ewen's son!"), biscuits, and "stork" with a snigger,

and up, up to Neil MacPhee's house
and the boys ashore with a song and a big bottle,
one with a shilling, one with a half-crown, one singing the 'Caiora'.

My Hogmanay skin-strip in my pocket,
and good is the smoke that comes from it:
it will go sun-wise round the children,
and especially round the housewife.

And down, down past the ditch,
and down, down past the ditch,
(where I had to have a pee),

my Hogmanay skin-strip in my pocket,
and good is the smoke that comes from it.

And how difficult the last lines were to remember,
and you so wee (Did anyone know them?, O God).

Chì thu nis iad ann an leabhar breagha,
(The Folksongs and Folklore of South Uist),
's mise cho diùid, le na briathran mòra:

Bean-an-taighe is i as fhiach e,
làmh a' riarachadh na Cullaig.
Rud beag de shochair an t-samhraidh
a' cumail geall air aig an aran.

Fosgail an doras is leig a-staigh mi!

Fosgail an doras is leig a-staigh mi!

Fosgail an doras is leig a-staigh mi!

You can now see them in the beautiful book,
(The Folksongs and Folklore of South Uist),
and I so shy, with the big words:

'Tis the housewife who deserves it,
here is the hand for the 'Hogmanay'.
A small thing of the good things of summer
To keep a promise got with the bread.

Open the door and let me in!

Open the door and let me in!

Open the door and let me in!

Wells and Stoves

(for Norman MacCaig)

Don't believe it, Norman!

Saxons tell us too many stories on the telly,
and sometimes we just say 'Aye, I ken' :

but
Oh to be at Crowdieknowe
when the last trumpet blaws,
stirring dull roots with spring rain!

This winter, my friend,
the water-pump broke down
and we pailed it for a week:
what a great splashing!

nothing
except the tin noise of the bucket
and the clean water from the holy well:

My God, Norman, it even sluices the shit away into the great polluted sea.

And as for electricity!

The cuts!

And instead, Gaelic beauty,
the stove, hissing away,
like all the Rayburns you ever saw
between Lochinver and Scalpay, ovens all ready and hot.

102

Fetch the peat!
Stir the fire!
Away with these firelighters!

Let's have the wood,
bleached by storms,
gathered from MacCaig's shore:
fur I tell ye: it's coming yet for aa' that!

Vietnam from Oban

My wee brother, aged 14,
wrote the essay that concluded:
'You've got to keep your eyes open in Vietnam.'

He was right, of course, in one way

about an American jungle
where napalm and chemicals had blinded millions
upon million of innocent children, even in Oban.

Skye After Edinburgh After Les Murray

We now arrive by car,
not donkey or horse-and-cart or bicycle,
having driven through Australian Scotland:
Glencoe was really astonishing – historical – yeah –
and Dalwhinnie just like the bush
before the Kyleakin ferry brought us home,
to ponder.

Scotland Is Not An Abstract Notion,
I declared to myself, afterwards,
looking out at the sprawl of the Cuillin
imagining that they were an Australian poet lying on her back.

Good God, it's amazing,
the smiles you can make, the metaphors you can invent,
the poems you can write by just seeing what's in front of your eyes.

So that was Les Murray:
a one-man bus tour,
a kangaroo,
a Free Church Minister
rolled – literally – into one.

And this is me –
a tiny sparrow on a swaying branch,
sometimes a seagull, sometimes a ranch.

By The Stove

it is very still and warm,

very Gaidhealach.

I sense your breath on the page,
very still, very blàth, and very beautiful.

Tick-tock

Return, my love,
from the Canadian Prairies.

For you should see what it's like here today:
very still, very warm, and very beautiful.

O, Canadian Moon,
that took our sisters,
what have you when I see the moon over Blàbheinn,
and last night the stars, the stars, Milky Way over Portree (of all places),
and the thunder, cracking out your name
completely, across the Highland skies.

Sometimes

I catch a glimpse of my wedding ring,

Celtic silver

shimmering in the dark.

Playtime

You are always there,

in those moments when I rise from prayer:

twirling in the playground with that smile
that is eternally carved in the palm
of Isaiah's hand.

The Widow's Offering

> "They all gave out of their wealth; but she, out of her poverty,
> put in everything – all she had to live on." (Mark: 12:24)

The Gaelic language is not an old boxer, flabby, remembering victories.

The greatest, without doubt, was Muhammed Ali
once floating like a butterfly and stinging like
the great pain in his moon eyes mumbling
oh Manila nights, Louiseville on the lovely lips,
Buddy Holly crackling like a fresh wireless,

men telling tales, the women at the washing,

the butterflies and the bees.

The Gaelic language is not an old boxer, flabby remembering victories.

After The Great Winter Storms

which have swept Ontario and Michigan and Balivanich

tourists arrive
with easels
and small brown dogs,

rocking wicker chairs making me externalise,
at last,

an endless Gaelic scream.

Aonghas na Beinne

Aidich.

Aigh, aidichidh mi.

Aidichidh mi
gur iomadh rud a dh'inns rèidio dhomh·
mu Iain Milne, mun Ghrèig agus mu Chomhairle nan Eilean.

Agus a-nis,
as deaghaidh BCCI
sgeulachd Aonghas na Beinne

a dh'atharraich an gràs.

Angus of the Ben

Confess.

Aye, I'll confess.

I'll confess
that radio has told me many things·
about John Milne, about Greece and about the Western Isles Council.

And now,
after BCCI,
the story of Angus of the Ben

transformed by grace.

Ag Iasgach a' Mhic-Meanmna

Air madainn Samhna,
a' tighinn tarsainn Bràigh na Teanga,
chunna mi tràlair a-muigh sa Chuan Sgìth.

Ring-netters m' eanchainn,
sgadan drithleannach mo chuimhne,
agus an cuan cho mòr, 's cho àlainn, 's cho farsaing.

Stad mi mionaid
aig Bealach an t-Sliachd
a' cur lìon thairis mo smuaintean.

An sluagh air an glùinean,
an Eaglais,
agus an cuan domhainn gar cuartachadh.

Fishing the Imagination

On a November morning,
coming over Upper Teangue,
I saw a trawler out in the Minch.

The ring-netters of my mind,
the glittering herring of my memory,
and the ocean so big, and so beautiful, and so wide.

I stopped for a moment
at the Brae of Humility
flinging a net over my thoughts.

The people on their knees,
the Church,
and the deep sea surrounding us.

Rote Learning

I must go down to the seas again
to the lonely sea and the sky
and all I ask is a tall ship
and a star to steer me by ...

After two years' observation,
I've just noticed that the Cuillin lies horizontally.

10 shillings half a pound
4 shillings one-third of a pound
7/6 three-eighth of a pound
12 shillings five-eights of a pound ...

as if it was like hammering nails into wood.

55 BC Julius Caesar invaded Britain
AD 80 Julius Agricolla led the Romans into Scotland
563 St Columba came to Iona
844 Kenneth MacAlpine became King over Dalriada, Pictland, Lothian and Strathclyde
1263 The Battle of Largs; The Hebrides became Scottish
1314 The Battle of Bannockburn
1513 The Battle of Flodden
1542 The Battle of Solway Moss; Mary Queen of Scots born
1560 Treaty of Leith
1587 The execution of Mary Queen of Scots
1588 The Spanish Armada
1603 The Union of the Crowns
1707 The Union of Parliaments

At which point Scottish History came to an end,
as if it had no connection with anything,
least of all with itself.

Millions of Highers, millions of graduates,
  millions of teachers, now millions of journalists.

I must go down to the seas again
to the lonely sea and the sky
and all I ask is a tall ship
and a star to steer her by ...

Do Ghabriel Garcia Marquez

Coileach

a' gairm

air mullach na sitig.

Mo bheannachd ort, a Ghabriel, airson an cat a chur air feadh na fìdhle.

For Gabriel Garcia Marquez

A cockerel

crowing

on top of the dung-heap.

My blessing on you, Gabriel, for bringing the chickens home to roost.

Farpais Rèidio nan Gaidheal

An-diugh,
's e Taobh-a-Deas Loch Baghasdail a tha an aghaigh Sgalpaigh

airson eàrlas clàr còig-nota-deug.

The Gaelic Radio Quiz

Today,
it's South Lochboisdale versus Scalpay

for a fifteen pound record token.

Abair Colonialism!

"Eskimoes have a very complicated language, and use one word where we would use a whole sentence. IGDLORSUAIIORTUSSARSIUMAVOQ is Eskimo for 'He wants to find someone to build him a house'." :
Something To Do, Puffin Books, 1966.

Tha deagh chuimhneam air,
's mi air an t-slighe dhan sgoil;
chìtheadh tu e aig ceann na bàthaich
le spaid agus bonaid 's e deànamh air a' mhachaire:
"Halò, bhalachaibh," dh'èigheadh e,
"feuch 's gun cum sibhse suas an sgoil, a-nis –
chan eil sian cho math ri foghlam!"

's fhad a dh'ionnsaich sinne breug às deaghaidh breug
(neo sgeul às deaghaidh sgeul)

bha esan shìos air a' mhachaire
a' treabhadh 's a' feannadh
a' feamanachadh 's ag innearadh
a' cur 's a' buain,

a cheann làn òran is eachdraidh
is seanchas a chual' e ann an Auckland
's ann an Cairo 's ann an Tierra del Fuego.

Esan air a' mhachaire a' seinn ris fhèin
's sinne anns na leabhraichean a' magadh air
IGDLORSSUALIORTUGSSARSIUMAVOQ.

Abair Colonialism!

"Eskimoes have a very complicated language, and use one word where we would use a whole sentence. IGDLORSUAIIORTUSSARSIUMAVOQ is Eskimo for 'He wants to find someone to build him a house'." :
Something To Do, Puffin Books, 1966.

I well remember him,
and I on my way to school:
you would see him at the end of the byre
with a spade and a bonnet, heading for the machair:
"Hello, lads", he would shout,
"see and keep up the school, now –
there's nothing like a good education."

and while we learned lie after lie
(or myth after myth)

he was down on the machair
ploughing and turning
harrowing and fertilizing
planting and harvesting,

his head full of songs and history
and tales that he'd heard in Auckland
and Cairo and Tierra del Fuego.

He was on the machair singing to himself
while we were in the books laughing at
IGDLORSSUALIORTUGSSARSIUMAVOQ.

Listening To An Emigrant

I was just saved by the skin of my teeth.

For I too could have gone to Australia,
joined the Ben Line
or the BBC

to be broken-hearted in a foreign land
watching the bush-heat shimmering,
yearning for the Luskentyre sand

and the sea and the spray and the silence.

Drawing A Picture

'Just watch a modern business meeting, and observe the notepads
full of doodles: how very familiar it all looks – from cave
walls!' : Language International Magazine, Vol 4 1992.

Hans Clausen, a friend,
says he can't remember his childhood
or whether he just had photographs of his childhood –
from bathing boy to punk, photograph after photograph after photograph.

And every letter begins like this:

Dear Hans,
We hope you are keeping well,
and enjoying the good weather. Mabel
and Stan have just returned
from their holiday in the Algarve
and they tell us the weather was wonderful.
Keep yourself warm and well wrapped up
and remember to send for anything you need for the winter,
yours sincerely, Uncle George and Auntie Peggy.

Then,
there was that awesome day we saw you young again
with your hair sleeked-back, and the suit so beautiful
brothers, all brothers, and wives and sisters and daughters
progenitors of a beautiful, unseen, generation.
Ah, beautiful.

Very beautiful.

On Saturday nights
Finlay's van arrived all-laden

and him sprinting sprucely up-and-down the tiny aisle
for many things that he's just-run-out-of, I'm afraid.

Photographs?, I ask myself.

After Epiphany, the Christmas cards hung in the village hall;
the first dance in the Junior Secondary;
lying on the brae above Glencoe;
pulled-into a layby on the Carnan Road;
you and me, my love, just out there.

(TV crews arrive constantly at my door,
setting-up that kitchen shot with the sea and the Cuillin;
'What I believe ......' I hear myself say,
believing every part, and trusting that a snow-flake would stay,
Ah, Gerinish; Ah, Glendale; Ah, Loch Skipport ......
...... all on drizzly mornings.)

At ten a.m., I sometimes think, the young housewife
moves about in negligee behind
the wooden walls of her husband's house.
I pass solitary in my car.

One great day, I resolve to myself,
I shall never utter another imperialist word
but advance into that cave
to draw you, in all your lined beauty,
with words that are, at last, entirely Gaelic,

mo ghràidh.

Shona

You sing across the generations of time,
like the whistle of a hydro-wire
from my own babyhood: mother and father snug
in the dark peat-room.

I sing of a river
green with sliced-rushes, beneath a wooden bridge:
Ah,waow,
the gentle race between the granity stuccos.

When gentle evenings circle me in Ord
I think of you, my love,
and your great knowledge of me diffused
through millions upon millions of clustered, singing, lights.

High-Tide. 5a.m. Ord.

We all had postcards on our mantlepieces
of those beautiful ships
that were all primary colours and funnels
sailing to such unbelieveable places –
New York! Brisbane! Rio de Janeiro!

How I desired!

Surely to goodness!

No matter what!

Listen! Listen!
Gather round! Come on! Come in!
Gather round! Listen!
In one of Alistair MacLeod's stories (strange how he always wears a suit!)
there is a very beautiful passage – really, a very beautiful passage.
It's Christmas Eve,
and the eldest son, Neil, (who's been working away on The Great Lakes),
has sent 'boxes of clothes' home from wondrous lake-places –
Cobourg, Toronto, St Catherines, Welland, Windsor, Sarnia and Sault Ste Marie.

They are all presents from Santa Claus for those who believe.

O, I believe!

I believe!

Can you hear me Alistair: oh (ohhhhhhhhhh), I believe!

This morning on the high-tide my home is an ocean-going liner

captained by Santa Claus and crewed by everybody who was ever righteous.
The first mate is Alistair MacLeod,
and the bosun is Dòmhnall Ailean Dhòmhnaill na Bainich
and the engineer is Dugie MacPhail
and the radio operator is my brother, my very own brother,
at last festooned in the flags of
The Clan Line, The Ben Line, The Star Line and The Red Line.

The cook is Mairi Mhòr nan Oran
and we have a resident bard (Sorley Mòr MacLean)
and a resident piper (Padraig Mòr MacCrimmon)
and a resident evangelist (Jesus Christ Himself)

and the great ship is sailing, on this high-tide,
into a morning chosen between sleep and an eternal, daily, waking.